Crochet Amigurumi Pig

Pig Amigurumi Crochet Patterns You'll Love

DEDICATION

Contents

Pig Doll

Size: about 6 inch.

GAUGE: 10 sc and 10 rows = 1.50 inch

MATERIALS

Crochet hook: Size 1.80 mm.

Worsted weight yarn (4 Ply):

- Dark Pink, Light Pink, Black

- Black bead 3 mm. (2) for eye.

Polyester fiberfill

Yarn needle

Scissors

INSTRUCTIONS

BODY: With Dark Pink

Rnd 1: Ch 2, 6 sc in second ch from hook; do not join. [6]

Rnd 2: Inc in each st around. [12]

Rnd 3: (Sc in next st, inc) rep around. [18]

Rnd 4: (Sc in next 2 sts, inc) rep around. [24]

Rnd 5: (Sc in next 3 sts, inc) rep around. [30]

Rnd 6: Sc in next 2 sts, inc, (sc in next 4 sts, inc) 5 times, sc in next 2 sts. [36]

Rnd 7: (Sc in next 5 sts, inc) rep around. [42]

Rnd 8: Sc in next 3 sts, inc, (sc in next 6 sts, inc) 5 times, sc in next 3 sts. [48]

Rnd 9-15: Sc in each st around.

Rnd 16: Sc in next 5 sts, dec, (sc in next 10 sts, dec) 3 times, sc in next 5 sts. [44]

Rnd 17: Sc in each st around.

Rnd 18: (Sc in next 9 sts, dec) rep around. [40]

Stuff Body firmly with polyester fiberfill as you work.

Rnd 19: Sc in each st around.

Rnd 20: Sc in next 4 sts, dec, (sc in next 8 sts, dec) 3 times, sc in next 4 sts. [36]

Rnd 21: Sc in each st around.

Rnd 22: (Sc in next 7 sts, dec) rep around. [32]

Rnd 23-24: Sc in each st around.

Fold in half, matching st on Front with next st on Back, working through both thicknesses, sc in next 16 sts, secure end, Finished.

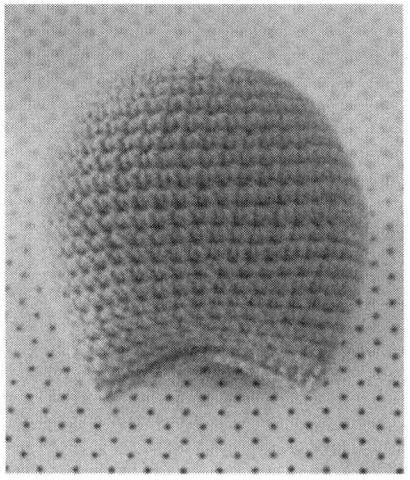

HEAD: With Dark Pink

Rnd 1: Ch 2, 6 sc in second ch from hook; do not join. [6]

Rnd 2: Inc in each st around. [12]

Rnd 3: (Sc in next st, inc) rep around. [18]

Rnd 4: (Sc in next 2 sts, inc) rep around. [24]

Rnd 5: (Sc in next 3 sts, inc) rep around. [30]

Rnd 6: Sc in next 2 sts, inc, (sc in next 4 sts, inc) 5 times, sc in next 2 sts. [36]

Rnd 7: (Sc in next 5 sts, inc) rep around. [42]

Rnd 8: Sc in next 3 sts, inc, (sc in next 6 sts, inc) 5 times, sc in next 3 sts. [48]

Rnd 9: (Sc in next 7 sts, inc) rep around. [54]

Rnd 10: Sc in next 4 sts, inc, (sc in next 8 sts, inc) 5 times, sc in next 4 sts. [60]

Rnd 11-22: Sc in each st around.

Stuff Head firmly with polyester fiberfill as you work.

Rnd 23: Sc in next 4 sts, dec, (sc in next 8 sts, dec) 5 times, sc in next 4 sts. [54]

Rnd 24: (Sc in next 7 sts, dec) rep around. [48]

Rnd 25: Sc in next 3 sts, dec, (sc in next 6 sts, dec) 5 times, sc in next 3 sts. [42]

Rnd 26: (Sc in next 5 sts, dec) rep around. [36]

Rnd 27: Sc in next 2 sts, dec, (sc in next 4 sts, dec) 5 times, sc in next

2 sts, sl st in next st. [30]

Finish off, leaving a long end for sewing.

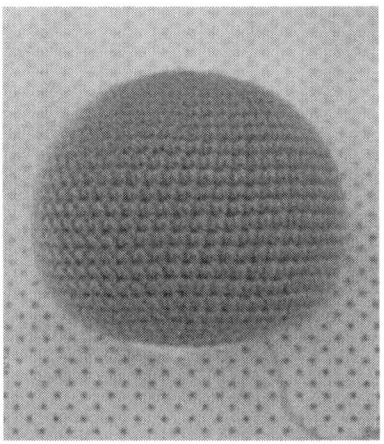

Put Head on Body, sew around in Rnd 5 of Body.

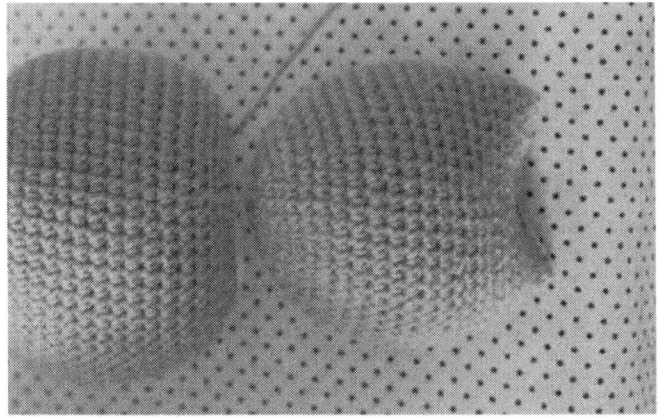

Using Black yarn sewing follow the photo below

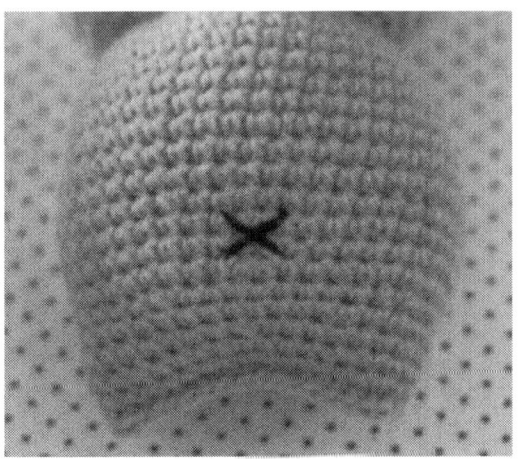

NOSE: With Light Pink

Rnd 1: Ch 6, sc in back ridge of second ch from hook, sc in next 3 chs, 3 sc in next ch, working in free loops of beginning ch, sc in next 3 chs, 2 sc in last ch, join with sl st to first st. [12]

Rnd 2: Ch 1, inc in same st, sc in next 4 sts, inc, inc, sc in next 4 sts, inc, join with sl st to first st. [16]

Rnd 3: Ch 1, sc in same st, inc, sc in next 4 sts, inc, sc in next 2 sts, inc, sc in next 4 sts, inc, sc in next st, join with sl st to first st. [20]

Rnd 4: Ch 1, sc in same st, sc in next st, inc, sc in next 4 sts, inc, sc in next 4 sts, inc, sc in next 4 sts, inc, sc in next 2 sts, join with sl st to first st. [24]

Finish off, leaving a long end for sewing.

Put Nose on Head, sew between Rnds 16 and 22 of Head.

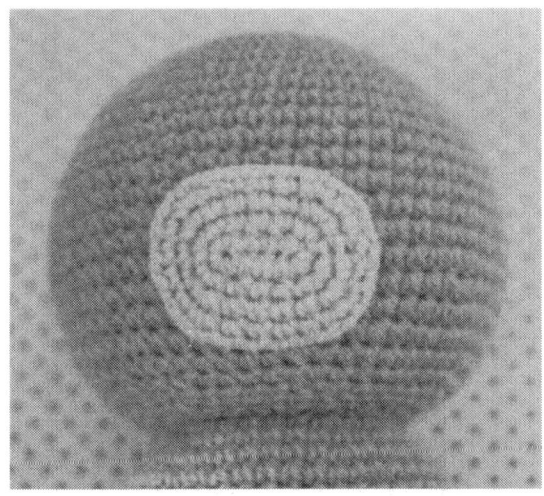

Using Black yarn sewing follow the photo below

EAR: With Dark Pink (Make 2)

Rnd 1: Ch 2, 6 sc in second ch from hook; do not join. [6]

Rnd 2: Inc in each st around. [12]

Rnd 3: (Sc in next st, inc) rep around. [18]

Rnd 4: (Sc in next 5 sts, inc) rep around. [21]

Rnd 5-7: Sc in each st around.

Fold in half, matching st on Front with next st on Back, working through both thicknesses, sc in next 10 sts, Finish off, leaving a long end for sewing.

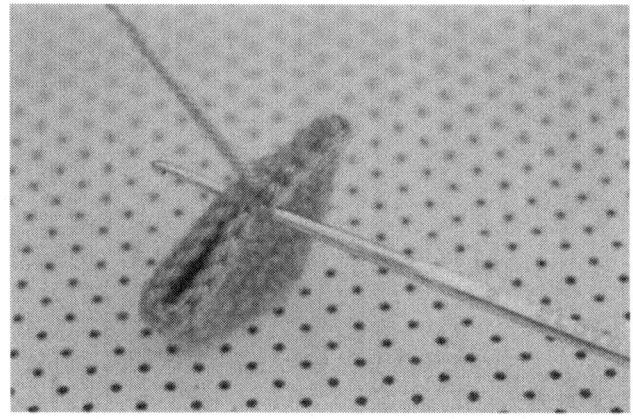

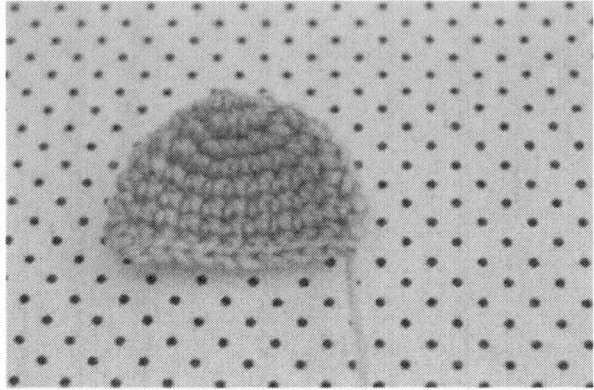

Put Ear on Head, sew between Rnd 8 and 16 of Head.

ARM: With Dark Pink (Make 2)

Rnd 1: Ch 2, 4 sc in second ch from hook; do not join. [4]

Rnd 2: Inc in each st around. [8]

Rnd 3: (Sc in next st, inc) rep around. [12]

Rnd 4-5: Sc in each st around.

Rnd 6: (Sc in next 3 sts, inc) rep around. [15]

Rnd 7: Sc in next 15 sts, sl st in next st.

Finish off, leaving a long end for sewing.

Put Arm on Body, sew between Rnd 6 and 11 of Body.

Stuff Arm firmly with polyester fiberfill as you work.

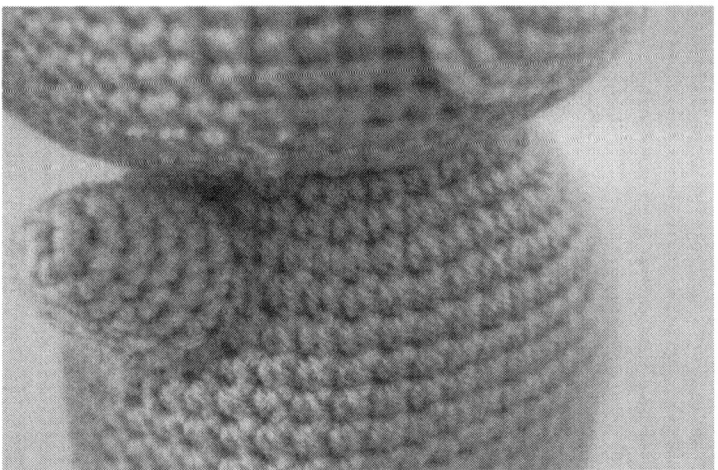

Little Pig

MATERIALS

DK (8ply) weight Drops Cotton Light (100% cotton; 50g/105m) – 2
colors

crochet hook 3 or 3.5 mm

polyester fiberfill

safety eyes (Ø 6mm)

some thread for stitching the nose

darning and embroidery needles

Abbreviations:

sc – single crochet, st(s) – stitch(es), rep – repeat

Work in continuous rounds. Do not join or turn unless otherwise instructed. It would be wise to use a stitch marker and place it in the first stitch of each round to mark the beginning of it.

INSTRUCTIONS

HEAD

Crocheted from top to bottom.

1: Start 6 sc in a magic ring.

2: Work 2 sc in each st around [12]

3: (Sc in next st, 2 sc in next st) rep 6 times [18]

4: (Sc in each of next 2 sts, 2 sc in next st) rep 6 times [24]

5: (Sc in each of next 3 sts, 2 sc in next st) rep 6 times [30]

6: (Sc in each of next 4 sts, 2 sc in next st) rep 6 times [36]

7: (Sc in each of next 5 sts, 2 sc in next st) rep 6 times [42]

8-16: Sc in each st around

Fasten safety eyes between rounds 12. and 13. Insert the first eye between them, then count 3 holes to the left and insert the second eye in the next hole. Close the washers from the inside of the piece.

17: (Sc in each of next 5 sts, sc2tog) rep 6 times [36]

18: (Sc in each of next 4 sts, sc2tog) rep 6 times [30]

19: (Sc in each of next 3 sts, sc2tog) rep 6 times [24]

20: (Sc in each of next 2 sts, sc2tog) rep 6 times [18]

Fill the head with fiberfill.

EAR (make 2)

1: Start 6 sc in a magic ring.

2: 1 sc in each st around

3: (Sc in next st, 2 sc in next st) rep 3 times [9]

4: (Sc in the next 2 sts, 2 sc in next st) rep 3 times [12]

5: (Sc in next st, 2 sc in next st) rep 6 times [18]

6-8: Sc in each st around

9: (Sc2tog) rep 9 times [9]

Attach the ears on the head.

MUZZLE

1: Start 6 sc in a magic ring.

2: Work 2 sc in each st around [12]

3: (Sc in next st, 2 sc in next st) rep 6 times [18]

4: Working in the back loops only, sc in each st around

Sew the muzzle in it's place. Add a tiny bit of stuffing before closing the seam. Stitch the nose.

LEGS AND BODY

Start with crocheting the legs and then join them, so they smoothly become the body.

1: Start 6 sc in a magic ring.

2: Work 2 sc in each st around [12]

3: (Sc in the next 3 sts, 2 sc in next st) rep 3 times [15]

4-7: Sc in each st around

8: Switch to contrasting color. Sc in each st around

Leave a yarn tail about 20 cm and cut the yarn. Make another leg similar to the first one.

NB! DO NOT BIND OFF THE SECOND LEG.

9: Now join the two legs. While using the yarn of the second leg sc in each of 15 sts around the first leg. Continue 15 sc around the second leg. In the end of the round you have joined the legs into one piece and you have 30 sc.

Close the hole between the legs using the short yarn tail left for the first leg.

10: Sc in each st around [30]

11: (Sc in the next 8 sts, sc2tog) rep 3 times [27]

12-13: Sc in each st around

14: (Sc in the next 7 sts, sc2tog) rep 3 times [24]

15-16: Switch back to main color. Sc in each st around

Stuff the legs and continue adding stuffing.

17: (Sc in the next 6 sts, sc2tog) rep 3 times [21]

18-19: Sc in each st around

20: (Sc in the next 5 sts, sc2tog) rep 3 times [18]

21: Sc in each st around

Sew the head to the body.

ARM

1: Start 6 sc in a magic ring.

2: Work 2 sc in each st around [12]

3-4: Sc in each st around

5: (Sc in the next 2 sts, sc2tog) rep 3 times [9]

6: Sc in each st around

Add some stuffing into the tip of the arm.

7: (Sc in the next st, sc2tog) rep 3 times [6]

8: Sc in each st around

Attach the arms to the body.

TAIL

Ch 8. Sc in the second stitch from hook. Work 2 sc in each of the next sts.

Attach the tail to the body.

Stitch suspenders using the contrasting color.

Crochet Along Pig

MATERIALS

Red Heart Comfort Color Code: 3133

4.5mm hook - use a smaller hook if you see gaps in your stitches

blunt end yarn needle for sewing

scissors

100% polyester stuffing

felt, paint, buttons, or yarn for eyes or safety eyes (I used a 10mm safety eye)

This pattern uses the following stitches:

st = stitch

sc = single crochet

hdc = half double crochet

sl st = slip stitch

2tog = crochet 2 stitches together

BLO = back loop only

f/o = finish off

INSTRUCTIONS

Starting at the top of the head working down to bottom of body:

1) magic circle with 6sc (6)

2) 2sc in each st (12)

3) 1sc then 2sc in next st (18)

4) 1sc in next 2st then 2sc in next st (24)

5) 1sc in next 3st then 2sc in next st (30)

in next st

6) 1sc then 2sc in next st (45)   *1sc in next st 2sc in next st. cont round 45 sts*

7-15) 1sc in each st for 9 rows

16) 2sc in next 6st, 1sc in next 6st, 2sc in next 6st, 1sc in next 27st (57)

17-18) 1sc in each st for 2 rows

19) (1sc in next 30st) then for the remaining st to the marker, 1sc in next 7st then 2tog (54)

20) 1sc in next 7st then 2tog (48)

21) 1sc in next 4st then 2tog (40)

22) 1sc in next 3st then 2tog (32)

23) 1sc in each st for 1 row

24) 1sc in next 2st then 2tog (24)

25) 1sc in next 2st then 2tog (18)

26) 1sc in each st for 1 row

27) 2sc in each st (36)

stuff the head, make sure to fill out those cheeks! You can add more stuffing as needed over the next few rows

28-30) 1sc in each st for 3 rows

31) 1sc in next 5st then 2sc in next st (42)

32-34) 1sc in each st for 3 rows

35) 1sc in next 5st then 2tog (36)

36) 1sc in each st for 1 row

37) 1sc in next 4st then 2tog (30)

38) 1sc in next 3st then 2tog (24)

39) 1sc in next 2st then 2tog (18)

begin to stuff the body

40) 1sc then 2tog (12)

stuff more as needed

41) 1sc then 2tog (8)

stuff more as needed

42) 2tog twice and f/o. Weave yarn tail in and out the remaining stitching and pull tight to close the gap. Knot off and hide yarn tail in body.

Muzzle:

1) magic circle with 6sc (6)

2) 3sc in first st, 1sc in next 2st, 3sc in next st, 1sc in next 2st (10)

3) 1sc then 2sc in next st (15)

1sc in next st then 2sc in next st
cont round

4) 1sc in next 2st, 2sc in next st, 3sc in next st, 1sc in next 5st, 3sc in next st, 2sc in next st, 1sc in next 4st (21)

5) 1sc in each of the BLO for 1 row

6-7) 1sc in each st for 2 rows

sl st next st and f/o leaving a long tail for sewing. Add in the nostrils before sewing muzzle to head. Sew most of the muzzle in place then stuff before sewing on completely.

Mouth:

1) magic circle with 6sc (6) begin with a long starting tail that you can sew into the head

2) ch1 and turn, 1sc then 2sc in the next st (9)

f/o leaving a long tail for sewing

Glue in a piece of red felt for the tongue after the mouth has been sewn in place

Ears:

1) magic circle with 6sc (6)

2) 1sc then 2sc in next st (9)

3) 1sc in each st

4) 1sc in the next 2st then 2sc in next st (12)

5) 1sc in each st

6) 1sc in next 3st then 2sc in next st (15)

7) 1sc in next 4st then 2sc in next st (18)

8-9) 1sc in each st for 2 rows

sl st next st and f/o leaving a long tail for sewing.

Arms:

1) magic circle with 6sc (6)

2) 2sc in each st (12)

3) 1sc in the next 3st then 2sc in the next st (15)

4-6) 1sc in each st for 3 rows

7) 2tog 3 times then 1sc in the next 9st (12)

8) 2tog twice then 1sc in the next 8st (10)

9-16) 1sc in each st for 8 rows

17) 1hdc in next 5st then sl st next st and f/o leaving a long tail for sewing. Stuff hand, lightly stuff arm.

Legs

1) magic circle with 6sc (6)

2) 2sc in each st (12)

3) 1sc then 2sc in next st (18)

4) 1sc in next 2st then 2sc in next st (24)

5-7) 1sc in each st for 3 rows

8) (2tog then 1sc in next st, repeat 6 times) 1sc in next 6st (18)

9) (2tog then 1sc in next st, repeat 4 times) 1sc in next 6st (14)

10) 1sc in the next 5st then 2tog (12)

11-22) 1sc in each st for 12 rows

sl st and f/o leaving a long tail for sewing. Stuff & shape foot and stuff leg.

Tail:

1) ch16 - begin with a long starting tail that you can sew into the body when done

2) 1sc then 2tog

f/o leaving a tail for sewing.

The tail should naturally curl but if not then hold one end of the tail and twist the other end.

Assembly:

If you assemble the doll in the order I give you then you will not have to worry so much about centering the different parts as much. The time in which the pieces are sewn in are listed in the video order just above the pattern (scroll up)

1) add in the indents for the eyes in between the 12th and 13th row with about 6 or 7 st between them. View video on how I did this. Time noted in the video order above.

2) glue in the safety eyes or add in buttons

3) Sew the arms on - sew 1 row down from the neck. Sew the top of the hdc to the body

4) sew on the legs. Turn the doll upside down and pin the legs in place then whip stitch the top edge of the legs to the body. View the video on how to do this.

5) sew on the tail

6) sew on the muzzle

place top of muzzle just above the 16th row, use lots of pins so it doesn't move around when you sew it in place

5) sew in the mouth

6) sew on the ears

7) click here for the dress and vest pattern

8) enjoy your pig!

Piggy Amigurumi

MATERIALS

Acrylic yarn in beige, cream, coffee-brown, pastel yellow and sea green

Crochet thread in black

2 x 4mm blue brads

Pink felt

Tools

3mm hook

Darning needle

Polyester fiberfill

INSTRUCTIONS

Description:

Princess P (short for Peanut) is a sweet, well-mannered little girl. She loves ice cream but mommy has just put her on a month-long diet. How nice it would be if she had a friend or two

Abbreviations

Ch: chain

Sc: single crochet

Dc: double crochet

Inv dec: invisible decrease

Head

With beige yarn:

Round 1: Sc 6 in magic ring {6}.

Round 2: [Inc] around {12}.

Round 3: [Inc, sc 1] around {18}.

Round 4: [Inc, sc 2] around {24}.

Round 5: [Inc, sc 3] around {30}.

Round 6: [Inc, sc 4] around {36}.

Round 7: [Inc, sc 5] around {42}.

Round 8: [Inc, sc 6] around {48}.

Round 9: [Inc, sc 7] around {54}.

Round 10-19 (10 rounds altogether): Sc around {54}.

Round 20: [Inv dec, sc 7] around {48}.

Round 21: [Inv dec, sc 6] around {42}.

Round 22: [Inv dec, sc 5] around {36}.

Round 23: [Inv dec, sc 4] around {30}.

Round 24: [Inv dec, sc 3] around {24}.

Round 25: [Inv dec, sc 2] around {18}.

Stuff head.

Round 26: [Inv dec, sc 1] around {12}.

Round 27: [Inv dec] around {6}.

Fasten off and leave a long tail to make eye indentations.

Eye indentations

Using the long tail end from the head, bring it up off-center to a spot below Round 13. Make a horizontal backstitch and bring the yarn back down to the bottom of the head. Gently tug to create an indentation. Repeat on the other side. There should be 9 stitches in between. Bring yarn to the bottom of the head and trim excess.

Snout

With beige yarn:

Round 1: Sc 5 in magic ring {5}.

Round 2: [Inc] around {10}.

Round 3: Sc around in back loop only {10}.

Clean faster off and leave a long tail for sewing.

Ears

Make 2 with beige yarn:

Round 1: Sc 3 in magic ring {3}.

Round 2: [Inc] around {6}.

Round 3: [Inc, sc 1] around {9}.

Round 4: [Inc, sc 2] around {12}.

Round 5-6 (2 rounds altogether): Sc around {12}.

Fasten off and leave a long tail for sewing.

Arms

Make 2 starting with coffee-brown yarn:

Round 1: Sc 6 in magic ring {6}.

Round 2-6 (5 rounds altogether): Change to beige yarn. Sc around {6}.

Fasten off and leave a long tail for sewing.

Legs

Make 2 starting with coffee-brown yarn:

Round 1: Sc 7 in magic ring {7}.

Round 2-4 (3 rounds altogether): Change to beige yarn. Sc around {7}.

Fasten off and leave a long tail for sewing.

Stuff lightly.

Body

With sea green yarn:

Round 1: Sc 6 in magic ring {6}.

Round 2: [Inc] around {12}.

Round 3: [Inc, sc 1] around {18}.

Round 4-11 (8 rounds altogether): Sc around {18}.

Fasten off and leave a long tail for sewing.

Stuff body.

Skirt

You will be surface-crocheting (counter-clockwise) onto the body. To start, turn the body piece upside down. With cream yarn on your hook:

Round 1: Sc 19{19}. (this will fall below Round 5 of the body piece)

Round 2: Sl st to first st. Continue sc around {19}.

Round 3: *4 hdc, sl st in next st, repeat from * 9 more times.

Fasten off and weave in ends.

Crown

With pastel yellow yarn:

Round 1: Ch 19 {19}.

Round 2: Sl st to first st. Continue sc around {19}.

Round 3: Sc around {19}.

Round 4: *Sc in the next 4 sc, ch 1, turn, sc2together, sc 1, ch 1, turn, sc2together, ss to next st, repeat from * 3 more times.

Fasten off and leave a long tail for sewing. Weave in other excess yarn ends.

Assembly

Sew snout onto head below Round 14.

Glue on blue brads for the eyes, below Round 15. They should be about 3-4 stitches away from the nose.

With black crochet thread, sew on the nostrils and eyelids with backstitches.

Sew body onto head.

Sew on arms and legs.

Sew on ears and crown.

Cut two pink felt circles and glue onto the cheeks.

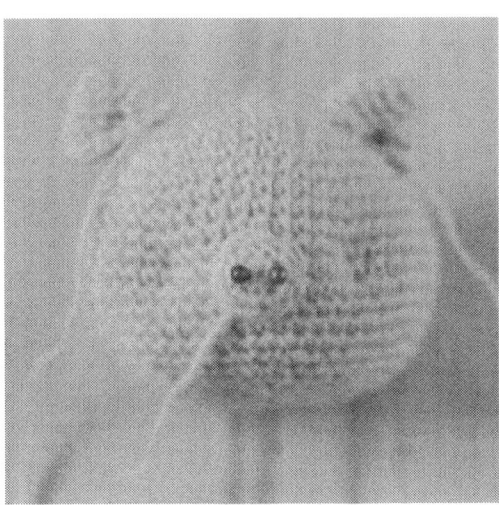

Pin pieces into place before sewing.

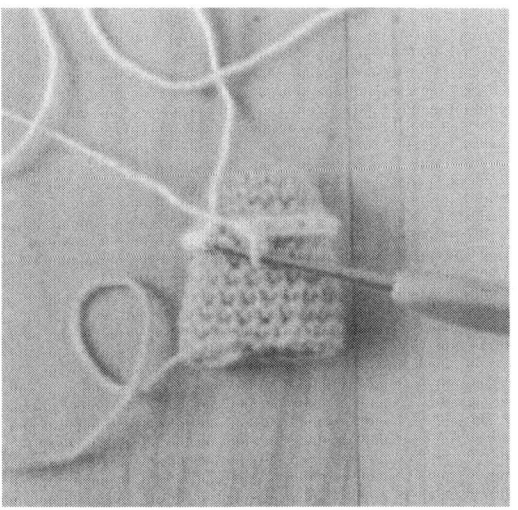

Turn body piece upside down. Surface-crochet the skirt directly onto the body piece.

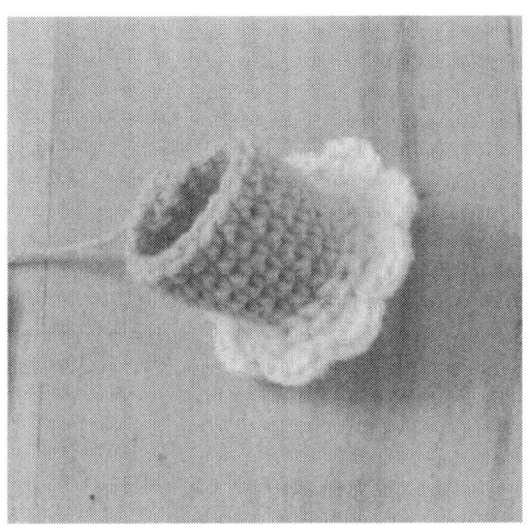

The skirt should have pretty frills like this.

Sew on the rest of the body parts. Make different poses for Princess P, if you like.

Amigurumi Pig

MATERIALS

Acrylic yarn in light and dark pink color (i have used 4ply/ sport weight acrylic yarn and 3mm crochet hook)

Little bit of blue, yellow and green yarn for flower

Crochet hook (according to the size of your yarn)

Poly fiber fill

Tapestry needle

6 mm safety eyes or flat back black beads for eyes

A small amount of pink felt

Black embroidery thread

This pattern is written in US English terms and worked in continuous rounds unless stated otherwise

ch - chain

sc - single crochet

sl st - slip stitch

dc - double crochet

dec - sc 2 together

rep ** - repeat stitches between **

INSTRUCTIONS

Head:

Using pink color yarn,

R1: 6 sc in magic ring (6)

R2: 2sc in each st (12)

R3: *sc in next st, 2 sc in next st*, rep **(18)

R4: *sc in next 2 st, 2sc in next st*, rep ** (24)

R5: *sc in next 3 st, 2sc in next st*, rep ** (30)

R6: *sc in next 4 st, 2sc in next st*, rep ** (36)

R7-11: sc in each stitch (36)

R12: *sc in next 4 st, dec 1 in next st*, rep ** (30)

R13: *sc in next 3 st, 1 dec in next st*, rep** (24)

R14: *sc in next 2 st, 1 dec in next st*, rep** (18)

R15: *sc in next st, 1 dec in next st*, rep** (12)

Stuff firmly and Fasten off leaving a tail for sewing

If using safety eyes, insert them between R10 and R11

Ears: (Make 2)

R1: 6 sc in magic ring (6)

R2: *sc in next st, 2 sc in next st*, rep** (9)

R3: *sc in next 2 st, 2 sc in next st,* rep** (12)

R4: sc around (12)

Fasten off, leaving a tail for sewing.

Snout: with dark pink color yarn,

R1: 6 sc in magic ring (6)

R2: 2 sc in each st (12), fasten off leaving a tail for sewing.

With black thread, embroider two vertical lines on the snout.

Arms: (Make 2)

R1: 6 sc in magic ring (6)

R2-7: sc around (6)

Fasten off leaving a tail for sewing.

Legs: make 2

R1: 6 sc in magic ring (6)

R2: *sc in next st, 2sc in next*, rep ** (9)

R3-5: sc in each st (9)

Fasten off the first leg.

Do not cut off the yarn on the second leg and chain 3 and join it to the first leg.

R6: sc around the 9 sts of first leg, sc in next 3 ch, sc in next 9 sts of second leg and sc in next 3 ch (24)

R7-12: sc around (24)

R13: *sc in next 6 st, dec 1 in next st*, rep ** (21)

R14: *sc in next 5 st, dec 1 in next st*, rep ** (18)

R15: *sc in next 4 st, dec 1 in next st*, rep ** (15)

R16: *sc in next 3 st, dec 1 in next st*, rep** (12)

Stuff firmly and fasten off leaving a tail for sewing

Tail:

ch 8, 2 sc in 2nd chain from hook, 2 sc in next 4 chain, sc in next 2 chain. Fasten off, leaving a long tail for sewing.

Flower:

with yellow yarn, 5 sc in magic ring and sl st to the first st

switch to blue color, *ch 1, 2 dc, ch 1 and sl st in the same st, and sl st to the next st*, rep **

Leaf:

with green yarn, ch 5, *dc in 3rd ch from hook, hdc in next and sl st in last ch*, ch 5 again and rep **

and sew the leaf to the flower.

Assembling:

Attach the body to the head.

Attach ears on either side of the head.

Sew on the snout onto the lower middle portion of the head.

Attach the arms to the body.

Attach the tails at the back.

Sew on the flower to the head.

Cut a small heart shape from pink felt and glue it near the belly.

And your little pig is ready!

Peppa and George Pig

MATERIALS

You can either use crochet cotton or baby yarn, using a 2.5mm hook or 8 ply yarn using a 3 mm hook

For Peppa's dress use a hook ½ mm bigger than the size of hook used for the rest of the body

Tapestry needle

Hobbyfill

Stitch marker or safety pin

You can use pipe cleaners to fill arms

Safety eyes (or you can crochet these)

Note:

This pattern is worked in continuous rounds (instead of joined rounds)

The ears and tail are worked in rows

To get size difference between Peppa and George, either use different size hooks (eg 3.5mm for Peppa and 3mm for George) or alternatively, use 8 ply on Peppa and 4 ply on George

Abbreviations:

mr = mr

sc = single crochet (US single crochet, not UK single crochet)

inc = increase

dec = decrease

ch = chain

tbl = through back of loop

* * = repeat

F/o = 1 slip stitch and fasten off

INSTRUCTIONS

HEAD (pink)

row 1 mr 8 sc (8)

row 2 2 inc (16)

row 3 *1 sc, inc 1* (24)

row 4 *2 sc 1 inc* (32)

row 5 *6 sc tbl, 1 dec tbl* (28)

rows 6-12 1sc in each sc

row 13 *1 sc 1 inc* (4 times), 12 sc, *1 inc, 1 sc* (4 times) (36) row 14 *2 sc 1 inc* (4 times), 12 sc, *1 inc, 2 sc* (4 times) (44)

row 15 *3 sc 1 inc* (4 times), 12 sc, *1 inc, 3 sc* (4 times) (52)

rows 16-17 1 sc in each sc

row 18 *3 sc 1 dec* (4 times), 12 sc, *1 dec, 3 sc* (4 times) (44)

place safety eyes if using them

rows 19 to 20 sc in each sc

row 21 *2 sc 1 dec* (x4), 12 sc, *1 dec, 2 sc* (4 times) (36)

rows 22 to 24 sc in each sc

row 25 *4 sc, one dec* (30)

row 26 sc in each sc

row 27 *2 sc, 1 dec* (23)

row 28 *1 sc, one dec* (16)

Fill head

row 29 8 dec (8) f/o

BODY (pink)

row 1 mr 8 sc

row 2 inc (16)

row 3 *1 sc 1 inc* (24)

row 4 *2 sc 1 inc* (32)

row 5 *1 inc, 3 sc* (40)

row 6 *4 sc 1 inc* (48)

rows 7 to 13 sc in each sc

row 14 *2 sc, 1 dec* (36)

row 15 *6 sc, 1 dec* 4 times, 4 sc (32)

row 16 *1 dec, 5 sc* 4 times, 4 sc (28)

row 17 *4 sc 1 dec* 4 times, 4 sc ((24)

row 18 *1 dec, 3 sc* 4 times, 4 sc (20)

Continue for Peppa:

change to red for dress and bigger crochet hook

row 19 sc in each sc

Turn and crochet in the opposite direction continuing with the red

row 1 sc in each sc (20)

row 2 *3 sc 1 inc* (25)

row 3 *1 inc, 4 sc* (30)

row 4 *5 sc, inc 1* (35)

row 5 *6 sc 1 inc* (40)

row 6 *2 sc, inc 1* 13 times, 1 sc (53)

rows 7 to 16 sc in each sc, f/o

Finish stuffing and sew to head

Continue for George:

row 19 sc in each sc (20)

start filling body with stuffing

row 20 10 dec (10) f/o

Finish stuffing and sew to head

EARS (pink)

chain 11

row 2 skip first chain and sc in each chain (10)

break yarn, fold over to create a horseshoe shape, sew edges together

FINGERS (4) (pink)

row 1 mr 6 sc

rows 2 to 3 sc in each sc f/o

ARMS (pink)

row 1 mr 6 sc

rows 2 to 3 sc in each sc

row 4 *1 sc, inc 1* (9)

rows 5 to 20 sc in each sc f/o

SHOES (BLACK)

row 1 mr 6 sc

row 2 inc in each sc

row 3 *5 sc 1 inc*

rows 4 to 10 sc in each sc

row 11 *5 sc 1 dec*

row 12 *2 sc 1 dec*

rows 13 to 14 sc in each sc

row 15 4 dec

Fill before hole becomes too small

LEGS (pink)

row 1 mr 10 sc

rows 2 to 14 sc in each sc

TAIL (pink)

row 1 8 ch

row 2 3 sc in each chain stitch

BLUSHES (darker pink)

row 1 mr 6 sc

row 2 inc in each sc

NOSTRILS (darker pink)

row 1 mr 6 sc

Both blushers, as are the nostrils of the nose can be made of felt.

Printed in Great Britain
by Amazon